Table of Contents

Week 1: All God's Promises

Questions to Discuss:

1) Think about and describe how your prayers – both HOW you pray and WHAT you pray FOR – have changed throughout your life.

_____

_____

Verses to Meditate on:

All God's Promises are Yes and Amen in Jesus

19 For the Son of God, Jesus Christ, who was preached among you by us—by me, Silvanus, and Timothy—was not Yes and No, **but in Him was Yes. 20 For all the promises of God in Him are Yes, and in Him Amen**, to the glory of God through us. 21 Now He who establishes us with you in Christ and has anointed us is God, 22 who also **has sealed us and given us the Spirit in our hearts as a guarantee.** *(2 Corinthians 1:18-22)*

Jesus: The Amen

Rev 3:14 **The Amen, the faithful and true Witness**, the Beginning of the creation of God.

God, the Amen, Keeps Covenant

"Know therefore that the LORD your God, He is God, the faithful God, which keeps covenant and mercy with them that love Him and keep His commandments to a thousand generations." *(Deuteronomy 7:9) "Faithful God" literally means "God the Amen"*

_____

_____

_____

_____

_____

_____

_____

Every Spiritual Blessing… in Christ

3 Blessed be the God and Father of our Lord Jesus Christ, **who has blessed us with every spiritual blessing** in the heavenly places **in Christ.** *(Ephesians 1:3)*

These Blessings Will Come on You

2 **All these blessings will come on you and accompany you** if you obey the Lord your God:
3 You will be **blessed in the city and blessed in the country.** 4 The **fruit of your womb will be blessed,** and **the crops of your land and the young of your livestock**—the calves of your herds and the lambs of your flocks. 5 **Your basket and your kneading trough will be blessed.** 6 You will be **blessed when you come in and blessed when you go out.**
7 The Lord will grant that **the enemies who rise up against you will be defeated before you.** They will come at you from one direction but flee from you in seven.
8 The Lord will send **a blessing on your barns and on everything you put your hand to.** The Lord your God will bless you in the land he is giving you. 9 The Lord will establish you as **his holy people,** as he promised you on oath, if you keep the commands of the Lord your God and walk in obedience to him. 10 Then **all the peoples on earth will see that you are called by the name of the Lord, and they will fear you.** 11 **The Lord will grant you abundant prosperity**— in the fruit of your womb, the young of your livestock and the crops of your ground—in the land he swore to your ancestors to give you.
12 **The Lord will open the heavens, the storehouse of his bounty**, to send rain on your land in season and to **bless all the work of your hands.** You will **lend to many nations** but will borrow from none. 13 **The Lord will make you the head, not the tail.** If you pay attention to the commands of the Lord your God that I give you this day and carefully follow them, **you will always be at the top, never at the bottom.** *(Deut 28:1-14)*

Week 1: Notes

Week 2: Old and New Covenant

Questions to Discuss:

Like Family Feud: What are the top 5 things which you have heard a Christian "should do" and top 5 things you have heard which a Christian "shouldn't do"? Ask yourself, "Why do we hear these things most often?"

	Old Covenant (Mosaic)	New Covenant
Covenant Transmission	John 1:17a For **the law was given** through Moses;	John 1:17b **Grace and truth came** through Jesus Christ.
Still in Effect	Hebrews 8: 13 When He said, "A new covenant," **He has made the first obsolete.**	Hebrews 7:18 For, on the one hand, there is a setting aside of a former commandment because of its weakness and uselessness 19 (for the Law made nothing perfect), **and on the other hand there is a bringing in of a better hope, through which we draw near to God.**
God's Presence	Hebrews 9:6 the priests are continually entering the outer tabernacle performing the divine worship, 7 but into the second, **only the high priest enters once a year,** not without taking blood, which he offers for himself and for the sins of the people committed in ignorance.	Hebrews 10:19 Therefore, brethren, since **we have confidence to enter the holy place by the blood of Jesus,** 20 by a new and living way which He inaugurated for us through the veil, that is, His flesh, 21 and since we have a great priest over the house of God, **22 let us draw near with a sincere heart in full assurance of faith,**
Qualification	Deut 28:1 If you **fully obey** the Lord your God and **carefully follow all his commands** I give you today, the Lord your God will set you high above all the nations on earth. 2 All these blessings will come on you and accompany you **if you obey the Lord your God…**	4 For **Christ is the end of the law for righteousness to everyone who believes.** Ephesians 2:8 For **by grace you have been saved through faith;** and that not of yourselves, it is **the gift of God;**
Sin	Hebrews 10:3 But in those sacrifices **there is a reminder of sins year by year.** 4 For it is impossible for the blood of bulls and goats to take away sins.	Hebrews 10:17 "And **their sins and their lawless deeds I will remember no more."** 18 Now where there is forgiveness of these things, there is no longer any offering for sin.
Perfection	Hebrews 7:19 (**for the Law made nothing perfect),**	Hebrews 10:14 For by one offering **He has perfected for all time those who are sanctified.**

Blood	Hebrews 9:19 For when every commandment had been spoken by Moses to all the people according to the Law**, he took the blood of the calves and the goats,** with water and scarlet wool and hyssop, and sprinkled both the book itself and all the people, 20 saying, **"This is the blood of the covenant which God commanded you."** 21 And in the same way he sprinkled both the tabernacle and all the vessels of the ministry with the blood. 22 And according to the Law, one may almost say, all things are cleansed with blood, and **without shedding of blood there is no forgiveness.** Exodus 24:8 So Moses took the blood and sprinkled it on the people, and said, **"Behold the blood of the covenant,** which the Lord has made with you in accordance with all these words."	Hebrews 9:11 But when Christ appeared as a high priest of the good things to come, He entered through the greater and more perfect tabernacle, not made with hands, that is to say, not of this creation; 12 and **not through the blood of goats and calves, but through His own blood,** He entered the holy place once for all, having obtained eternal redemption. 13 For if the blood of goats and bulls and the ashes of a heifer sprinkling those who have been defiled sanctify for the cleansing of the flesh, 14 **how much more will the blood of Christ, who through the eternal Spirit offered Himself without blemish to God, cleanse your conscience from dead works to serve the living God?** Luke 22:20 And in the same way He took the cup after they had eaten, saying, "This cup which is poured out for you is **the new covenant in My blood.**
Sacrifice Frequency	Hebrews 10:1 For the Law, since it has only a shadow of the good things to come and not the very form of things, can never, by the same sacrifices **which they offer continually year by year,** make perfect those who draw near. 2 Otherwise, would they not have ceased to be offered, because the worshipers, having once been cleansed, would no longer have had consciousness of sins?	Hebrews 10:12 But He, **having offered one sacrifice for sins for all time,** sat down at the right hand of God.
Blessings	Deut 28:2 **All these blessings will come upon you and overtake you if you obey the Lord your God:** 3 Blessed shall you be in the city, and blessed shall you be in the country. 4 Blessed shall be the offspring of your body and the produce of your ground and the offspring of your beasts, the increase of your herd and the young of your flock. 5 Blessed shall be your basket and your kneading bowl. 6 Blessed shall you be when you come in, and blessed shall you be when you go out.	Ephesian 1:3 Blessed be the God and Father of our Lord Jesus Christ, **who has blessed us with every spiritual blessing in the heavenly places in Christ,** 4 just as He chose us in Him before the foundation of the world, that we would be holy and blameless before [d]Him 2 Corinthians 1:20 For as many as are the promises of God, **in Him they are yes; therefore also through Him is our Amen** to the glory of God through us.
Curses	Deut 28:15 But it shall come about, **if you do not obey the Lord your God, to observe to do all His commandments and His statutes** with which I charge you today, **that all these curses will come upon you and overtake you:** 16 Cursed shall you be in the city, and cursed shall you be in the country. 17 Cursed shall be your basket and your kneading bowl. 18 Cursed shall be the offspring of your body and the produce of your ground, the increase of your herd and the young of your flock. 19 Cursed shall you be when you come in, and cursed shall you be when you go out. Galatians 3:10 **For as many as are of the works of the Law are under a curse;** for it is written, "Cursed is everyone who does not abide by **all things written in the book of the law,** to perform them."	Galatians 3:13 **Christ redeemed us from the curse of the Law, having become a curse for us**—for it is written, "Cursed is everyone who hangs on a tree"—

Week 2: Notes

Week 3: Near to God

Week 3

Questions to Discuss:

1) On a scale of 1-10, would you say that on a normal day God seems close or far away? Why?

_____

_____

Verses to Meditate on:

Heb 8:8 "Behold, days are coming, says the Lord, when I will effect **a new covenant**... 11 "And they shall not teach everyone his fellow citizen, And everyone his brother, saying, 'Know the Lord,' **For all will know Me, From the least to the greatest of them.**

Through the New Covenant we Draw Near

Hebrews 7:19 On the other hand there is a bringing in of a better hope, **through which we draw near to God.**

And We Know the Love of Christ

Eph 3:17 that you, being rooted and grounded in love, 18 may be able to comprehend with all the saints what is the breadth and length and height and depth, 19 and **to know the love of Christ which surpasses knowledge,** that you may be filled up to all the fullness of God.

Know (ginskō) – to know, especially through personal experience

And We Experience His Love

1 John 3:16 This is how we KNOW **what love is - Jesus Christ laid down his life for us**.

Draw Near with Confidence

Heb 10:19 Therefore, brothers, **since we have confidence to enter the holy places by the blood of Jesus**, 20 by the **new and living way** that he opened for us through the curtain, that is, through his flesh, 21 and since we have a great priest over the house of God, 22 **let us draw near with a true heart in full assurance of faith,** with our hearts sprinkled clean from an evil conscience and our bodies washed with pure water. 23 Let us hold fast the confession of our hope without wavering, for **he who promised is faithful.**

Come to the Father

John 14:1 "Do not let your heart be troubled; believe in God, believe also in Me. 2 In My Father's house are many dwelling places; if it were not so, I would have told you; for I **go to prepare a place for you. 3 If I go and prepare a place for you,** I will come again and **receive you to Myself, that where I am, there you may be also.** 4 And you know **the way** where I am going." 5 Thomas *said to Him, "Lord, we do not know where You are going, **how do we know the way?**" 6 Jesus *said to him, "**I am the way, and the truth, and the life; no one comes to the Father but through Me.**"

With Jesus, Where He Is

John 17: 24 Father, I desire that they also, whom You have given Me, **be with Me where I am**, so that they may see My glory which You have given Me, **for You loved Me before the foundation of the world.**

Eph 2:4 But God, being rich in mercy, **because of His great love with which He loved us...6 raised us up with Him, and seated us with Him in the heavenly places in Christ Jesus.**

Week 3: Notes

_____

_____

_____

_____

_____

_____

_____

_____

_____

_____

Week 4: Abide in Me, and I in You

Questions to Discuss:

1) What is your favorite wedding scene from a movie?

_____

_____

2) In what ways is the relationship between Jesus and the Church similar to a marriage?

_____

_____

Verses to Meditate on:

New Covenant Promise – His Spirit in Us

Ex 36:26 Moreover, I will give you a new heart and **put a new spirit within you**; and I will remove the heart of stone from your flesh and give you a heart of flesh. 27 **I will put My Spirit within you.**

One Spirit with Him

1 Corinthians 6:15 Do you not know that your bodies are members of Christ? ...17 **But the one who joins himself to the Lord is one spirit with Him**... 19 Or do you not know that your body is a **temple of the Holy Spirit who is in you**, whom you have from God, and that you are not your own? 20 For you have been bought with a price.

_____

_____

_____

_____

_____

_____

This Mystery is Great

Ephesians 5:25 Husbands, love your wives, just **as Christ also loved the church and gave Himself up for her, 26 so that He might sanctify her,** having cleansed her by the washing of water with the word, 27 that He might present **to Himself** the church in all her glory, having no spot or wrinkle or any such thing; but that she would be **holy and blameless**....31 For this reason a man shall leave his father and mother and shall be joined to his wife, and **the two shall become one flesh**. 32 **This mystery is great;** but I am speaking with reference to **Christ and the church.**

One – As Jesus and the Father are One

John 17:20 "I do not ask on behalf of these alone, but **for those also who believe in Me through their word**; 21 that they may all be one; even as You, Father, are in Me and I in You, **that they also may be in Us**, so that the world may believe that You sent Me. 22 The glory which You have given Me I have given to them, that they may be one, **just as We are one**; 23 **I in them and You in Me**, that they may be perfected in unity, so that the world may know that **You sent Me, and loved them, even as You have loved Me.**

You in Me, I in You - Abide in My Love

John 15:**4 Abide in Me, and I in you**. As the branch cannot bear fruit of itself unless it abides in the vine, so neither can you unless you abide in Me. 5 **I am the vine, you are the branches; he who abides in Me and I in him,** he bears much fruit, for apart from Me you can do nothing...**9 Just as the Father has loved Me, I have also loved you; abide in My love.**

Week 4: Notes

_____

_____

_____

_____

_____

_____

_____

_____

_____

_____

_____

Week 5: Known By Him

Questions to Discuss:

1) Tell about someone famous or influential that you know or have had an encounter with?

_____

_____

_____

Verses to Meditate on:

Friends (or a Brother) in High Places

Genesis 42:1 Now Jacob saw that there was grain in Egypt, and Jacob said to his sons, "Why are you staring at one another?" 2 He said, "Behold, I have heard that there is grain in Egypt; go down there and buy some for us from that place, so that we may live and not die."...

6 Now **Joseph was the ruler over the land**; he was the one who sold to all the people of the land. And Joseph's brothers came and bowed down to him with their faces to the ground. 7 **When Joseph saw his brothers he recognized them...**

50:19 But Joseph said to them, "Do not be afraid, for am I in God's place? 20 As for you, **you meant evil against me, but God meant it for good in order to bring about this present result, to preserve many people alive.**

_____

_____

_____

_____

_____

_____

_____

Known By God

Galatians 4:9 But now that you have come to know God, or **rather to be known by God**…

Jeremiah. 1:5 "Before I formed you in the womb **I knew you**..."

Chosen by Him

John 13:18b I know the ones I have chosen;

Ephesian 1:4 He chose us in him before the foundation of the world, that we should be holy and blameless before him.

He Thinks about You

Ps 139:17 **How precious also are Your thoughts to me, O God! How vast is the sum of them**! 18 If I should count them, **they would outnumber the sand.**

He Understands You

Heb 4 15 For we do not have a high priest who cannot sympathize with our weaknesses, **but One who has been tempted in all things as we are, yet without sin.** 16 Therefore let us **draw near** with confidence to the throne of grace, so that we may receive mercy and **find grace to help in time of need.**

Psalm 139

1 O Lord, You have searched me and **known me. 2 You know when I sit down and when I rise up; You understand my thought from afar.**3 You scrutinize my path and my lying down, **And are intimately acquainted with all my ways.**4 Even before there is a word on my tongue, Behold, O Lord, You know it all.5 You have enclosed me behind and before, And laid Your hand upon me. 6 **Such knowledge is too wonderful for me;** It is too high, I cannot attain to it.

7 Where can I go from Your Spirit? Or where can I flee from Your presence? 8 If I ascend to heaven, **You are there;** If I make my bed in Sheol, behold, **You are there.** 9 If I take the wings of the dawn, If I dwell in the remotest part of the sea, 10 Even there Your hand will lead me, And **Your right hand will lay hold of me.** 11 If I say, "Surely the darkness will overwhelm me, And the light around me will be night," 12 **Even the darkness is not dark to You**, And the night is as bright as the day. Darkness and light are alike to You.

13 For You formed my inward parts; You wove me in my mother's womb. 14 I will give thanks to You, for **I am fearfully and wonderfully made; Wonderful are Your works,** And my soul knows it very well.15 My frame was not hidden from You, When I was made in secret, And skillfully wrought in the depths of the earth; **16 Your eyes have seen my unformed substance; And in Your book were all written the days that were ordained for me**, when as yet there was not one of them.

Week 5: Notes

Week 6: Forgiveness

Questions to Discuss:

1) As a kid, did you ever make a mess and try to clean it up or fix it without your parents knowing?

_____

_____

2) You have heard the saying "forgive and forget". Do you think it is possible that God forgets our sins?

_____

_____

_____

Verses to Meditate on:

A New Covenant

"Behold, days are coming," declares the Lord, "when I will make **a new covenant** with the house of Israel and with the house of Judah, 32 not like the covenant which I made with their fathers in the day I took them by the hand to bring them out of the land of Egypt, **My covenant which they broke, although I was a husband to them**," declares the Lord. 33 "But this is the covenant which I will make with the house of Israel after those days," declares the Lord, "I will put My law within them and on their heart I will write it; and I will be their God, and they shall be My people. 34 They will not teach again, each man his neighbor and each man his brother, saying, 'Know the Lord,' for **they will all know Me**, from the least of them to the greatest of them," declares the Lord, "**for I will forgive their iniquity** (guilt), **and their sin** (to miss, go wrong) **I will remember no more.**" _(Jeremiah 31:31)_

_____

_____

_____

_____

_____

_____

Sins Taken Away - In HIM There is No Sin

You know that **He appeared in order to take away sins**; and **in Him** there is **no sin**. (1 John 3:5)

Now, little children, **abide in Him**, so that when He appears, we may have confidence and **not shrink away from Him in shame** at His coming. *(1 John 2:28)*

Behold, the Lamb of God

The next day he saw Jesus coming to him and said, "Behold, the **Lamb of God who takes away the sin of the world!** *(John 1:29)*

So **Christ was sacrificed** once **to take away the sins** of many people. *(Hebrews 9:28)*

Transgressions Removed

As far as the **east is from the west**, So far has **He removed our transgressions** (rebellious acts) **from us**. *(Psalm 103:12)*

Released From our Sins

To Him **who loves us** and **released** (loosed, untied) **us from our sins by His blood.** *(Rev 1:5)*

Love Keeps No Record of Wrong

4 Love is patient, love is kind. ... 5 **it keeps no record of wrongs.** (I Cor. 13:4,5)

See Hebrews 11: **No record of their wrong, just their faith and what they did by faith.**

Week 6: Notes

_____

_____

_____

_____

_____

_____

_____

_____

_____

_____

Week 7: Salvation

Questions to Discuss:

1) Tell about a time when you were stuck and in need of outside help. (For example, your car broke down.)

_____

_____

2) What things come to mind when you think of the word "salvation" or being "saved"?

_____

_____

Verses to Meditate on:

Not to Condemn but to Save

For God so loved the world that he gave his one and only Son, **that whoever believes in him shall not perish but have eternal life.** 17 For God did not send his Son into the world to condemn the world, but **to save the world through him.** *(John3:16)*

Jesus/Joshua – The Lord Saves

Hebrew word: yesha - deliverance, help, salvation
Name of "Jesus" derived from this Hebrew root

She will give birth to a son, and you are to give him the name Jesus, because **he will save his people from their sins."** *(Matthew 1:21)*

Greek Word: sozo - to make safe FROM danger, peril, judgment; to make safe FOR or unto health, benefit, victory. (Saved, Healed, Delivered.)

_____

_____

_____

_____

_____

_____

_____

Your Faith Has Healed/Saved You

20 Just then a woman who had been subject to bleeding for twelve years came up behind him and touched the edge of his cloak. 21 She said to herself, "If I only touch his cloak, **I will be healed.**" 22 Jesus turned and saw her. "Take heart, daughter," he said, "**your faith has healed you.**" And **the woman was healed** at that moment. *(Matt 9:20-22)*

Salvation Only in Jesus

12 **Salvation is found in no one else**, for there is no other name under heaven given to mankind **by which we must be saved.**" *(Acts 4:12)*

By Grace You Were Saved, Through Faith

2 As for you, **you were dead in your transgressions and sins,** 2 in which you used to live when you followed the ways of this world and of the ruler of the kingdom of the air, the spirit who is now at work in those who are disobedient. 3 All of us also lived among them at one time, gratifying the cravings of our flesh and following its desires and thoughts. Like the rest, we were by nature deserving of wrath. **4 But because of his great love for us, God, who is rich in mercy, 5 made us alive with Christ even when we were dead in transgressions— it is by grace you have been saved.** 6 And God raised us up with Christ and seated us with him in the heavenly realms in Christ Jesus, 7 in order that in the coming ages he might show the incomparable riches of his grace, expressed in his kindness to us in Christ Jesus. **8 For it is by grace you have been saved, through faith— and this is not from yourselves, it is the gift of God— 9 not by works, so that no one can** boast. (Ephesians 2:1-9)

Saved Through the Washing of Rebirth

4 But when the kindness and love of God our **Savior** appeared, 5 **he saved us**, not because of righteous things we had done, but because of his mercy. **He saved us through the washing of rebirth and renewal by the Holy Spirit, 6 whom he poured out on us generously through Jesus Christ our Savior**, 7 so that, having been **justified by his grace**, **we might become heirs** having the hope of eternal life.

Week 7: Notes

_____

_____

_____

_____

_____

_____

_____

_____

_____

_____

Week 8: Redemption

Questions to Discuss:

1) What is one of the favorite purchases you have ever made?

_____

_____

2) What are some of the difference between being a slave and a son/daughter (or heir)?

_____

_____

Verses to Meditate on:

Redeemed with Precious Blood

You were not redeemed with perishable things like silver or gold **from your futile way of life** inherited from your forefathers, **but with precious blood,** as of a lamb unblemished and spotless, **the blood of Christ.** For He was foreknown before the foundation of the world, but has appeared in these last times **for the sake of you who through Him are believers in God,** who raised Him from the dead and gave Him glory, **so that your faith and hope are in God.** *(1 Peter 1:18-21)*

Redepmption:
A. Greek Definition: Redemption is the act of buying something back, or paying a price to return something to your possession.

B. Hebrew meaning - The release of people, animals or property from bondage through outside help. Only someone strong or rich can redeem.

_____

_____

_____

_____

_____

_____

_____

Redeemed to Receive Adoption

But when the fullness of the time came, **God sent forth His Son**, born of a woman, **born under the Law**, so **that He might redeem those who were under the Law, that we might receive the adoption as sons**. Because you are sons, God has sent forth the Spirit of His Son into our hearts, crying, "Abba! Father!" **Therefore you are no longer a slave, but a son; and if a son, then an heir through God.** *(Galatians 4:4-7)*

Redeemed from the Curse of the Law

Christ redeemed us from the curse of the Law, having become a curse for us—for it is written, "Cursed is everyone who hangs on a tree"— in order that in Christ Jesus the blessing of Abraham might come to the Gentiles, so **that we would receive the promise of the Spirit** through faith. *(Galatians 3:12-14)*

How Much More the Blood of Christ

But when Christ appeared as a high priest of the good things to come, He entered through the greater and more perfect tabernacle, not made with hands, that is to say, not of this creation; and not through the blood of goats and calves, **but through His own blood,** He entered the holy place once for all, **having obtained eternal redemption**. For if the blood of goats and bulls and the ashes of a heifer sprinkling those who have been defiled sanctify for the cleansing of the flesh, **how much more will the blood of Christ, who through the eternal Spirit offered Himself without blemish to God, cleanse your conscience from dead works to serve the living God?** For this reason **He is the mediator of a new covenant**, so that, since a death has taken place **for the redemption of the transgressions that were committed under the first covenant**, those who have been called may receive **the promise of the eternal inheritance.** *(Hebrews 9:11-15)*

Zacharias' Prophecy

Luke 1:67-80 And his father Zacharias was filled with the Holy Spirit, and prophesied, saying: "Blessed be the Lord God of Israel, **For He has visited us and accomplished redemption for His people,** And has raised up **a horn of salvation for us.** In the house of David His servant— As He spoke by the mouth of His holy prophets from of old— **Salvation from our enemies,** And from the hand of all who hate us; To show mercy toward our fathers,**And to remember His holy covenant, The oath which He swore to Abraham our father,** To grant us that we, **being rescued** from the hand of our enemies, **Might serve Him without fear, In holiness and righteousness before Him all our days.** "And you, child, will be called the prophet of the Most High; For you will go on before the Lord to prepare His ways; To give to His people **the knowledge of salvation. By the forgiveness of their sins, Because of the tender mercy of our God,With which the Sunrise from on high will visit us, To shine upon those who sit in darkness and the shadow of death,**To guide our feet into **the way of peace.**" And the child continued to grow and to become strong in spirit, and he lived in the deserts until the day of his public appearance to Israel.

Boaz – Kinsman Redeemer

Ruth 4:9-17 Then Boaz said to the elders and all the people, "You are witnesses today that **I have bought from the hand of Naomi all that belonged to Elimelech and all that belonged to Chilion and Mahlon. Moreover, I have acquired Ruth the Moabitess,** the widow of Mahlon, to be my wife in order **to raise up the name of the deceased on his inheritance,** so that the name of the deceased will not be cut off from his brothers or from the court of his birth place; you are witnesses today." All the people who were in the court, and the elders, said, "We are witnesses. **May the Lord make the woman who is coming into your home like Rachel and Leah, both of whom built the house of Israel**; and may you achieve wealth in Ephrathah and **become famous in Bethlehem.** Moreover, may your house be like the house of Perez whom Tamar bore to Judah, through the offspring which the Lord will give you by this young woman." So Boaz took Ruth, and she became his wife, and he went in to her. And the Lord enabled her to conceive, and she gave birth to a son. **Then the women said to Naomi, "Blessed is the Lord who has not left you without a redeemer today, and may his name become famous in Israel.** May he also be to you a restorer of life and a sustainer of your old age; for your daughter-in-law, who loves you and is better to you than seven sons, has given birth to him." Then Naomi took the child and laid him in her lap, and became his nurse. The neighbor women gave him a name, saying, **"A son has been born to Naomi!"** So they named him Obed. **He is the father of Jesse, the father of David.**

Other Verses

Revelation 5:9-10 And they *sang a new song, saying,"Worthy are You to take the book and to break its seals; for You were slain, and **purchased for God with Your blood men from every tribe and tongue and people and nation.** "You have made them to be **a kingdom and priests** to our God; **and they will reign upon the earth.**"

Acts 20:28 Be on guard for yourselves and for all the flock, among which the Holy Spirit has made you overseers, to **shepherd the church of God which He purchased with His own blood.**

1 Corinthians 6:19-20 Or do you not know that your body is **a temple of the Holy Spirit who is in you, whom you have from God, and that you are not your own? For you have been bought with a price:** therefore glorify God in your body.

Week 8: Notes

Week 9: Fruitfulness

Questions to Discuss:

1) What do you think goes on in your heart vs. your mind?

_____

_____

2) Describe someone you know that you would say has a 'Fruitful' life?

_____

Verses to Meditate on:

Hearing and Receiving "The Word"

But these are the ones sown on good soil: They **hear the word** and **receive it** and **bear fruit**, one thirty times as much, one sixty, and one a hundred. *(Mark 4:20)*

So **faith comes from hearing**, and **hearing by the word of Christ**.*(Romans 10:17)*

Did you **receive** the Spirit by the works of the Law, or **by hearing with faith**? Are you so foolish? After beginning by means of the Spirit, **are you now trying to finish by means of the flesh?** *(Galatians 3:2-3)*

In the beginning was the **Word**, and the Word was with God, and **the Word was God**...12 as many as **received Him**, to them He gave **the right to become children of God**, [even] to those who **believe in His name...** 17For the law was given through Moses; **grace and truth came through Jesus Christ.** *(John 1:1, 12, 17)*

_____

_____

_____

_____

_____

_____

_____

Believing in Our Hearts = Righteousness

But what does it say? **"The word is near you, in your mouth and in your heart"**—that is, the word of faith which we are preaching, that if you confess with your mouth Jesus as Lord, and **believe in your heart that God raised Him from the dead,** you will be saved; **for with the heart a person believes, resulting in righteousness,** and with the mouth he confesses, resulting in salvation. For the Scripture says, **"Whoever believes in Him will not be disappointed."** *(Romans 10:8-11)*

The New Covenant: His Spirit in our Hearts

"This is the covenant that I will make with them. After those days, says the Lord:**I will put My laws upon their heart,**And on their mind I will write them." *(Hebrews 10:16)*

God has sent forth **the Spirit of His Son into our hearts**, crying, "Abba! Father!" *(Galatians 4:6)*

Fruit: Because His Peace Guards your Heart

15 But the seed on good soil… *(is those who)* **hear the word, retain it,** and **by persevering bear fruit.** *(Luke 8:15)*

And the **peace of God,** which surpasses all comprehension, **will guard your hearts and your minds in Christ Jesus.** *(Philippians 4:7)*

Fruit of the Spirit

But **the fruit of the Spirit is love, joy, peace,** patience, kindness, goodness, faith, 23gentleness, self-control; **against such things there is no law.** *(Gal 5:22-23)*

His Word(s) in Your Heart = Life

20 My son, **give attention to my words;** **Incline your ear** to my sayings. 21 Do not let them depart from your sight; **Keep them in the midst of your heart.** 22 For **they are life** to those who find them and **health to all their body.** 23 **Watch over your heart** with all diligence, **for from it flow the springs of life.** *(Prov 4:20-23)*

_____

_____

_____

_____

_____

_____

_____

_____

_____

Week 9: Notes

Week 10: Transformation

Questions to Discuss:

1) Tell about a time in your life when you changed a lot?

_____

_____

2) What are some technques that people try when they want to change something in their life?

_____

_____

Verses to Meditate on:

God Crowned Us With Glory

But one has testified somewhere, saying, "What is man, that You remember him? Or the son of man, that You are concerned about him? 7 "You have made him for a little while lower than the angels; **You have crowned him with glory and honor,** And have appointed him over the works of Your hands; 8 You have put all things in subjection under his feet. *(Hebrews 2:6-8)*

We Exchanged the Glory of God

21 For even though they knew God, they did not honor Him as God or give thanks, but they became futile in their speculations, and their foolish heart was darkened. 22 Professing to be wise, **they became fools, 23 and exchanged the glory of the incorruptible God for an image in the form of corruptible man and of birds and four-footed animals and crawling creatures."** *(Rom 1:21-23)*

All Fall Short of the Glory of God

For all have sinned and **fall short of the glory of God.** *(Romans 3:23)*

Jesus Gives Us His Glory

1 Jesus spoke these things; and lifting up His eyes to heaven, He said, "Father, the hour has come; **glorify Your Son, that the Son may glorify You,** 2 even as You gave Him authority over all flesh, that to all whom You have given Him, He may give eternal life. 3 This is eternal life, that they may know You, the only true God, and Jesus Christ whom You have sent. **4 I glorified You on the earth, having accomplished the work which You have given Me to do.** 5 Now, Father, **glorify Me together with Yourself, with the glory which I had with You before the world was....22 The glory which You have given Me I have given to them,** that they may be one, just as We are one; 23 I in them and You in Me, that they may be perfected in unity, so **that the world may know that You sent Me, and loved them, even as You have loved Me.** 24 Father, I desire that they also, whom You have given Me, be with Me where I am, so **that they may see My glory which You have given Me, for You loved Me before the foundation of the world.** *(John 17:1)*

God's Glory Replaces the Sun and Moon

And the city has no need of the sun or of the moon to shine on it, for **the glory of God has illumined it, and its lamp is the Lamb.** *(Rev 21:23)*

Transformed – From Glory to Glory

2 Cor 3:5 Our adequacy is from God, 6 who also made us adequate as servants of a new covenant, **not of the letter but of the Spirit;** for the letter kills, but the Spirit gives life. 7 But if the ministry of death, in letters engraved on stones, came with glory, so that the sons of Israel could not look intently at the face of Moses because of the glory of his face, fading as it was, 8 **how will the ministry of the Spirit fail to be even more with glory?** 9 For if the ministry of condemnation has glory, **much more does the ministry of righteousness abound in glory.** 10 For indeed what had glory, in this case has no glory because of the glory that surpasses it. 11 **For if that which fades away was with glory, much more that which remains is in glory.** 12 Therefore having such a hope, we use great boldness in our speech, 13 and are not like Moses, who used to put a veil over his face so that the sons of Israel would not look intently at the end of what was fading away. 14 But their minds were hardened; for until this very day at the reading of the old covenant the same veil remains unlifted, because it is removed in Christ. 15 But to this day whenever Moses is read, a veil lies over their heart; 16 but **whenever a person turns to the Lord, the veil is taken away.** 17 Now the Lord is the Spirit, and where the Spirit of the Lord is, there is liberty. 18 **But we all, with unveiled face, beholding as in a mirror the glory of the Lord, are being transformed into the same image from glory to glory, just as from the Lord, the Spirit.** *(John 16: 14-15)*

All Creation Will Be Set Free

That **the creation itself also will be set free from its slavery to corruption into the freedom of the glory of the children of God.** *(Romans 8:21)*

Week 10: Notes

_____

_____

_____

_____

_____

_____

_____

_____

_____

_____

Week 11: Streams of Living Water

Questions to Discuss:

1) What are some of the benefits of having God's Spirit in our hearts vs. having a list of laws that we read, memorize and meditated on?

_____

2) Read the passage from John 4 below and tell what do you think it means that if we drink of His water, we will never thirst again?

_____

Verses to Meditate on:

A Well of Living Water

There came a woman of Samaria to draw water. Jesus said to her, "Give Me a drink." For His disciples had gone away into the city to buy food. Therefore the Samaritan woman said to Him, "How is it that You, being a Jew, ask me for a drink since I am a Samaritan woman?" For Jews have no dealings with Samaritans. Jesus answered and said to her, **"If you knew the gift of God, and who it is who says to you, 'Give Me a drink,' you would have asked Him, and He would have given you living water."** She said to Him, "Sir, You have nothing to draw with and the well is deep; where then do You get that living water? You are not greater than our father Jacob, are You, who gave us the well, and drank of it himself and his sons and his cattle?" Jesus answered and said to her, "Everyone who drinks of this water will thirst again; **but whoever drinks of the water that I will give him shall never thirst; but the water that I will give him will become in him a well of water springing up to eternal life."** *(John 4:7-14)*

_____

_____

_____

_____

_____

_____

_____

_____

Living Water from Our Innermost Being

Now on the last day, the great day of the feast, Jesus stood and cried out, saying, **"If anyone is thirsty, let him come to Me and drink. He who believes in Me, as the Scripture said, 'From his innermost being will flow rivers of living water.'"** But this He spoke of **the Spirit, whom those who believed in Him were to receive**; for the Spirit was not yet given, because Jesus was not yet glorified. *(John 7:37-39)*

New Covenant - His Spirit Within Us

"But this is the covenant which I will make with the house of Israel after those days," declares the Lord, **"I will put My law within them and on their heart I will write it;** *(Jeremiah 31:33-34)*

The Letter Kills, the Spirit Gives Life

Our adequacy is from God, 6 who also made us adequate as servants of a **new covenant**, not of the letter but **of the Spirit; for the letter kills, but the Spirit gives life.** *(2 Corinthains 3:5-6)*

Fruit from the Treasure of Our Heart

For there is no good tree which produces bad fruit, nor, on the other hand, a bad tree which produces good fruit. **For each tree is known by its own fruit.** For men do not gather figs from thorns, nor do they pick grapes from a briar bush. **The good man out of the good treasure of his heart brings forth what is good; and the evil man out of the evil treasure brings forth what is evil; for his mouth speaks from that which fills his heart.** *(Luke 6:44-45).*

Week 11: Notes

_____

_____

_____

_____

_____

_____

_____

_____

_____

_____

Week 12: Reign in Life

Questions to Discuss:

1) What do you think it means to 'reign' or 'have dominion'?

_____

_____

2) *(Answer this question after completing the lesson)* What are examples in your life of 'sin' or 'death' reigning vs 'grace' or 'life' reigning (Romans 5:21)?

_____

_____

Verses to Meditate on:

Fill the Earth, Subdue it and Rule

27 God created man **in His own image, in the image of God He created him**; male and female He created them. 28 **God blessed them;** and God said to them, **"Be fruitful and multiply, and fill the earth, and subdue it; and rule** over the fish of the sea and over the birds of the sky and over every living thing that moves on the earth." *(Genesis 1:26-28)*

Death Reigned from Adam

Nevertheless **death reigned from Adam until Moses,** even over those who had not sinned in the likeness of the offense of Adam, who is a type of Him who was to come. *(Romans 5:14)*

_____

_____

_____

_____

_____

_____

Your Kingdom Come

9 "Pray, then, in this way:
'Our Father who is in heaven,
Hallowed be Your name.
**10 'Your kingdom come.
Your will be done,
On earth as it is in heaven.** *(Matt 6:9-10)*

Jesus–Far Above All Rule and Authority

Now judgment is upon this world; now the ruler of this world will be cast out. *(John 12:31)*

Jesus–Far Above All Rule and Authority

Eph 1:18 I pray that the eyes of your heart may be enlightened, so that you will know what is the hope of His calling, what are the riches of the glory of His inheritance in the saints, 19 and what is the surpassing greatness of His power toward us who believe. These are in accordance with the working of the strength of His might 20 which He brought about in Christ, when He raised Him from the dead and **seated Him at His right hand** in the heavenly places, 21 **far above all rule and authority and power and dominion, and every name that is named, not only in this age but also in the one to come.** 22 And He put **all things in subjection under His feet**, and gave Him as head over all things to the church, 23 which is His body, the fullness of Him who fills all in all. *(Eph 1:18-23)*

Raised and Seated With Him

Eph 2:4 But God, being rich in mercy, **because of His great love with which He loved us**, 5 even when we were dead in our transgressions, made us alive together with Christ (by grace you have been saved), 6 and **raised us up with Him, and seated us with Him in the heavenly places in Christ Jesus**. *(Eph 2:4-6)*

The Righteous Will Reign in Life

For if by the transgression of the one, death reigned through the one, **much more those who receive the abundance of grace and of the gift of righteousness will reign in life through the One, Jesus Christ.** 18 So then as through one transgression there resulted condemnation to all men, even so through one act of righteousness there resulted justification of life to all men. 19 For as through the one man's disobedience the many were made sinners, even so through the obedience of the One the many will be made righteous. 20 The Law came in so that the transgression would increase; but where sin increased, grace abounded all the more, 21 so that, **as sin reigned in death, even so grace would reign through righteousness to eternal life through Jesus Christ our Lord.** *(Romans 5:17-21)*

A Kingdom and Priests

And they *sang a new song, saying, "**Worthy are You** to take the book and to break its seals; for You were slain, and **purchased for God with Your blood men from every tribe and tongue and people and nation.** 10 "You have made them to be **a kingdom and priests to our God; and they will reign upon the earth.**" *(Rev 5: 9-10)*

_____

_____

_____

Week 12: Notes

_____

_____

_____

_____

_____

_____

_____

_____

_____

Week 13: "You Shall" vs "I Will"

Questions to Discuss:

1) What are some of the things you learned in the last 12 weeks of doing this study?

_____

_____

2) How have you changed in the last 12 weeks of doing this study?

_____

_____

Verses to Meditate on:

All God's Promises are Yes and Amen in Jesus

19 For the Son of God, Jesus Christ, who was preached among you by us—by me, Silvanus, and Timothy—was not Yes and No, **but in Him was Yes. 20 For all the promises of God in Him are Yes, and in Him Amen**, to the glory of God through us. 21 Now He who establishes us with you in Christ and has anointed us is God, 22 who also **has sealed us and given us the Spirit in our hearts as a guarantee.** *(2 Corinthians 1:18-22)*

God, the Amen, Keeps Covenant

"Know therefore that the LORD your God, **He is God, the faithful God, which keeps covenant.** *(Deuteronomy 7:9)* *"Faithful God" literally means "God the Amen"*

_____

_____

_____

_____

_____

_____

Old Covenant – You Shall/Shall Not

3 "**You shall** have no other gods before Me. 4 **"You shall not... 5 You shall not... 7 You shall not...8 Remember the sabbath** 9 Six days **you shall labor... you shall not** ...12 **Honor your father and your mother...** 13 **You shall not... 14 You shall not... 15 You shall not...16 You shall not 17 You shall not...** *(Ex 20:3-17)*

A New Covenant - I will

"Behold, days are coming," declares the Lord, "when **I will** make a new covenant with the house of Israel and with the house of Judah, 32 not like the covenant which I made with their fathers in the day I took them by the hand to bring them out of the land of Egypt, My covenant which they broke, although I was a husband to them," declares the Lord. 33 "But this is the covenant which **I will** make with the house of Israel after those days," declares the Lord, "**I will** put My law within them and on their heart **I will** write it; and **I will** be their God, and they shall be My people. 34 They will not teach again, each man his neighbor and each man his brother, saying, 'Know the Lord,' for they will all know Me, from the least of them to the greatest of them," declares the Lord, "for **I will** forgive their iniquity (guilt), and their sin (to miss, go wrong) **I will remember no more.**" *(Jeremiah 31:31)*

By Grace... Through Faith

1 And **you were dead** in your trespasses and sins, 2 in which you formerly walked according to the course of this world, according to the prince of the power of the air, of the spirit that is now working in the sons of disobedience. 3 Among them we too all formerly lived in the lusts of our flesh, indulging the desires of the flesh and of the mind, and were by nature children of wrath, even as the rest. 4 But God, being rich in mercy, **because of His great love with which He loved us**, 5 even when **we were dead** in our transgressions, **made us alive** together with Christ (by grace you have been saved), 6 and **raised us up with Him**, and **seated us** with Him in the heavenly places in Christ Jesus, 7 so that in the ages to come He might show the surpassing riches of His grace in kindness toward us in Christ Jesus. 8 For **by grace you have been saved through faith**; and that not of yourselves, **it is the gift of God**; 9 not as a result of works, so that no one may boast. 10 **For we are His workmanship**, created in Christ Jesus for good works, which God prepared beforehand so that we would walk in them. *(Eph 2:1-10)*

_____

_____

_____

_____

Week 13: Notes

Made in the USA
Middletown, DE
30 August 2019